Wherever the Sweet Breeze Blows

Wherever the Sweet Breeze Blows

Poems by

Liana Sakelliou

Translated by

Don Schofield

Cover design by Shay Culligan
Cover image by Elena Sheehan
Author photo by Stefanos Schultz

ISBN: 979-8-90146-702-2

Kelsay Books
502 South 1040 East, A-119
American Fork, Utah 84003
Kelsaybooks.com

For my son Stefanos

Also by the Author

Poetry

This Side of Eden, translators Angela Bratsou and Stavros Deligiorgis, Bucharest, Romania: Vinea, 2025.
Portrait Before Dark, translator Aliki Barnstone, San Antonio, Texas: Saint Julian Press, 2022.
Take Me Like a Photograph, translator David Connolly, Athens: Typothito, 2005.

Translations

Aliki Barnstone, *Eva: The Voices of an Imaginary Poet* (Editor and Translator), Athens: Vakhikon, 2023.
Brendan Kennelly, *The Blarney Stone* (Editor), Athens: Erato, 1992.
Emily Dickinson, *Because I Could Not Bear to Live Aloud* (Editor), Athens: Gutenberg, 2013.
Gary Snyder, *The Poetics and Politics of Place* (Editor), Athens: Odysseas, 1998.
H. D., *Introduction to the Trilogy* (Editor), Athens: Gutenberg, 1999.
Ralph Waldo Emerson, *The Man Against the Sky* (Editor), Athens: Gutenberg, 1994.

Criticism

Levertov's Poetry of Revelation, 1988–1998: The Mosaic of Nature and Spirit, Athens: Typothito, 1999.
Feminist Criticism on American Women Poets: An Annotated Bibliography 1975–1993, New York: Garland, 1994.
Denise Levertov: An Annotated Primary and Secondary Bibliography, New York: Garland, 1988.

Acknowledgements

Thank you to the following publications, in which versions of these poems previously appeared, sometimes with different titles:

Apple Valley Review: "Lessons for the Poros Naval Base"

Arkana: "Demosthenes the Athenian on Kalavria"

Barrow Street: "Living in Silver"

basalt: "Parthenis Visits the Monastery," "The Link with My Body," "The Boat and the Fish," "Portraits with Butterflies"

Circumference: "Menses and the Sea," "Vigil," "The Slaughter-houses," "Recording the Sacrifices," "Paint Store," "Temple of Poseidon, 1965"

Crazyhorse: "Tree of Life," "Bird of Death"

Ergon: "With a View of the Sea"

Euphony: "Balackla"

Ginosko: "Short History of a Deluge," "Coat of Arms," Watery Miracle"

Guesthouse: "Still Life with No Background"

The High Window (UK): "Springs," "Portraits with Butterflies," "Love Harbor," "Matina and the Story of Extermination"

Illuminations: "The Water of Life"

Los Angeles Review: "Raffaello Ceccoli's Icon, 1853," "The Gate," "Greta Garbo at Kyvelia," "The Conquest"

Maryland Literary Review: "Vagionia Delta"

The Mason Street Review: "The Source of Her Tears"

Oberon: "Film of an Engagement Party in a Lemon Orchard," "Descent into Hades"

Plume: "The Virgin's Miracles," "Since Childhood"

Poet Lore: "Festival of Dionysos," "Ghost in Black and White"

Rhino: "The Italian Circus on the Moraitiki Shore," "Marine Education at the Beginning of the Twenty-First Century"

Deep gratitude to all my friends and family for their island stories—their memories brought the history of Poros back to life.

Special thanks to Stavros Deligiorgis for his vital interest in my work, Don Schofield for his brilliant translations, Karine Leo Ancellin for her invaluable help with the publication, and, of course, to my husband, Bill Schultz—my daily inspiration and partner in all things writerly.

Contents

I. THE WATER OF LIFE

The Water of Life 21

II. SPRINGS

Springs 27
At the Gate to the Spring 30
Balackla 31
The Virgin's Miracles 32
Raffaello Ceccoli's Icon, 1853 33
Parthenis Visits the Monastery 34
The Well Inside the House 35
The Source of Her Tears 36
The Experience of Eros 37

III. TRUSTED COLORS

Portraits with Butterflies 41
Devil's Bridge 44
Giannis Scarlatos and Xanthoula Kouneli 45
Distributing the Fruit 46
Giannis Scarlatos's Engagement, 1952 47
Paint Store 48
The Annunciation (1907) 51
Kostis Parthenis Rowing 52
The Month of Departures 53
Still Life with No Background 54
The Fateful Summer of Ioannis Kapodistrias, 1831 55

Like a Midsummer Afternoon 56
Festival of Dionysos 57
The Italian Circus on the Moraitiki Shore 59
Merçi pour le Beau Sejour 60
The Boat and the Fish 61

IV. WITH A VIEW OF THE SEA

With a View of the Sea 65

V. THE PALACES

The Palaces 83
Temple of the Trident, 1976 85
Vagionia Delta 86
Temple of Poseidon, 1965 87
The God 88
Vigil 89
Recording the Sacrifices 90
Demosthenes the Athenian on Kalavria 93

V. HANDIWORK OF UNIQUE VALUE

Galini—His Last Strait 97
Guestbook 100
Cyclamen Graecum 102
Ghost in Black & White 103
Coat of Arms 104

Lessons for the Poros Naval Base 106
The Return 107
Matina and the Story of Extermination 108
The Magical LP 412 110
Canal 111
The Yard 112
What Glistened 113
Body in the Light 114
Living in Silver 115
Menses and the Sea 116
The Slaughterhouses 117
Tselevinia 118
Pentimento 119
Watery Miracle 120
Initiation 121
The Gate 122
Descent into Hades 123
Soirées Musicales 124
Marine Education at the Beginning of the Twentieth Century 125
Greta Garbo at Kyveleia 126
The Link with My Body 127
The Vegetable Gardens 128
The Geometry of Stone 129
Love Harbor 130
Tectonics 131
Short History of a Deluge 132
Bird of Death, April 21, 1967 133
The Conquest, July 21, 1969 135
Since Childhood 136
Cadenza 137

Eros and Thanatos, as She Felt It 138
Film of an Engagement Party in a Lemon Orchard 139
Tree of Life 141

Notes 143

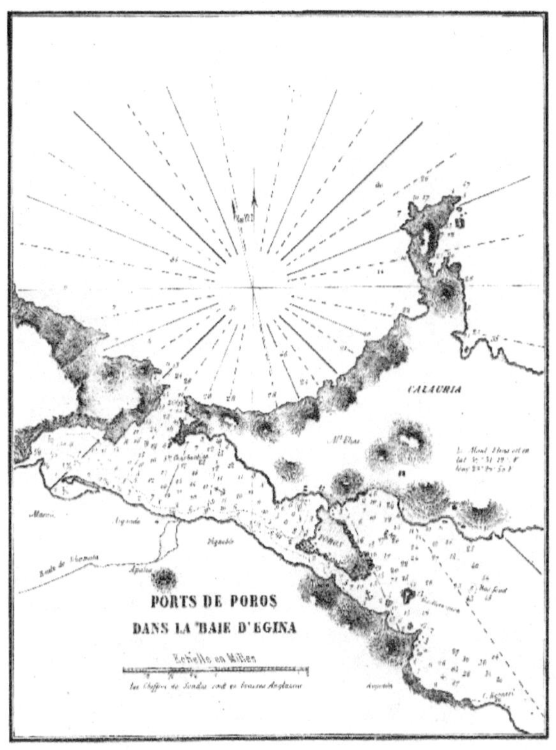

Located on the southwestern side of the Saronic Gulf,
50–100 meters from the Peloponnese,
in the province of Hydra and Troizinias,
part of the Municipality of Troizinias,
the island is comprised of two smaller islands—
Sfairia, stony and barren, where Poros Town is located,
and Kalavria, verdant with gardens and forests of firs
and other trees; a small isthmus connects the two islets.

—Miltiades Boukas, *Guide to Greece,* Athens 1875, pp. 306–7

I.

THE WATER OF LIFE

The Water of Life

The immortal waters flow and expel death
from the realm of the young. Forget the fever,
I tell you. At the monastery of the Orthodox monks
there's still hope. There the flowing waters
will dissolve all your melancholy.

*

1847: Argia Ceccoli, seventeen,
travels to the island of Kalavria,
disembarking with her father
at the monastery dock.

Abbot Nikiforos
lifts the iron-studded bolt high and opens the gate.
"I am infected," she mutters, looking askance
at the rows of cells behind him.

Raffaello readies hot compresses,
takes vials from his leather bag
and spreads thick straw on a wooden pallet
for her to lie down. He lifts her back slightly
so she can drink what he offers.

Through the narrow cell window
night is falling. Argia can't stop coughing.
He has taught her how to identify the deep red
of Pompeii on fire among the splotches
staining her embroidered handkerchief. Here,
at last, even if a Catholic,
Raffaello Ceccoli feels safe.

*

Holy Abbot, soothe the heartache that keeps gnawing
at my father, who shows his faith in your country
with paintings. On the slope of the Holy Rock,
hold the Greek banner high, spread wide
the red Communion cloth.

As I drink the life-giving water you offer
and my hair grows longer,
teach me endurance. Sacred Water,
stay alive within me.

*

Seasons slip by.
Thyme and heather blossom on the mountainside.
Martens dig deep tunnels at night.
Now Argia eats at the common table,
pronounces the admirals' names
on the gravestones. Wars will come again,
bodies of the young again will disappear.
Toll the bells mournfully.
Sono in pericolo, Signore!

*

Give me your hand, my child.
We will find the water's source, or else
the diviner will find it with his dowsing rod;
light will caress the solar clock,
nudge its saving hand toward your cell.

*

1849: Severe frost destroys the beehives

and citrus trees. The monastery
is driven to indigence.

Poverty makes us admit
our weakness, in the end
leaves us totally helpless.

*

June 11, 1849.
Of course all belongs to Her—
even my daughter is Hers.
She took her like a vengeful goddess.
So, when night falls
give the orphans her golden adornments,
her fine cotton socks,
her embroidered vest,
all her elaborate weavings.
While chanters grieve, give the mourners
rose-flavored Turkish delight.

*

He boards a boat.
Maybe somewhere in the middle of the sea
he'll remember the monastery.
Must he close the circle there? Maybe there
his wanderings were just beginning.

Little is known about the rest of his life.
Some say he returned to Naples,
others that he went to London
to exhibit the work of his students,
still others that he stayed in Athens

to paint the portrait of the king.
They all consider him a traveler, not a fugitive.

Again and again in his landscapes
he paints the poor and the holy,
shepherds and clergymen.

In the year 1853
he still believed that art
could work wonders. He returned
to the island at the height of spring,
put her remains in a box. Departing,
he left a gift, a painting in which Argia
is the Holy Mother and as a child,
the Holy Infant. On the base of a laver
he wrote in red:

"From the painter Raffaello Ceccoli
to the Monastery of the Life-Giving Spring,
in gratitude, 1853."

*

During a divine torrent, Nikiforos
remembered the beehives. Under the bridge,
where he meant to protect them,
the relentless waters swept him
and the bees away.

Under the icon on the wooden stand
he had wanted to finish
while the girl was still alive,
he carved his name and the year:
"Abbot N. Sakelliou, 1869."

II.

SPRINGS

Springs

In Hebrew we knew it as *âyîn*,
a pit for gathering water; as *mägộr*,
the source of life; its gushing water
as *mabbû-â;* as *Ain Sara* in ancient Hebron,
a spreading out; and in the city of Sychar
as a well where myriads
came to drink
and still they died.

We have also found it
in the desert of Baer-Sheva,
where the mother of Ishmael
met the Angel of the Lord—
the first Annunciation.

Hagar, poor soul, her story extraordinary,
was expelled with her infant.
She wandered the desert, thirsty
and dying, sobbing mournfully
until the Angel showed her the spring, bid her drink
and give water to her child.
Life returned to them.

Later we meet her as Aphrodite Pudica
wringing water from her hair with both hands.
Zephyros and Aura
shoved her up onto the shore
and she became Venus Marina.

Crouched there covered in salt,
her long hair flowing down,
Anadyomene Aphrodite
slowly rises from the waves.
Then Euploea, Pontia, Pelagia and immediately
hulls and fountains with spigots,
the giant tridacna—
all become wombs.

From deadly Baer-Sheva
until her full-bodied birth
in foam off Cyprus,
how did her soul hide in that shell,
and how did all this come to be
in that briny water?

Fishermen found her
as a rusted icon
in the crevice of a rock,
removed the barnacles of time
and the mastic wax she was encased in.

Mass hysteria followed,
new excavations
to find more icons,
an epidemic of dreams and lunacy—
is this image possessed?

Half gown, half sea;
half body, half cloud—
the dripping creature
has been captured!

Tides and lingering fog
can smell the precious icon.
The ripples of her veil waft fresh and damp.
Her cloak slowly opens
and contracts . . . .

Moon,
grace her with fertility.
Osiris give her the scepter.
Nereids, Water Nymphs, Goddess of Cyprus—
may you become One in this creature,
the Virgin Mother of all Springs.

At the Gate to the Spring

He kept going, the blind one,
looking hard to find, deep in the forest,
the Spring.

He heard God's voice,
drank it
and rejoiced.

Then he saw the water
bubbling up
crystal clear.

Balackla

The emperors vacationed at Balackla,
its palaces with springs
known for their fish
swimming in holy water.

Fish still fall there,
it's believed, jumping

from a monk's
frying pan—

such an untamed miracle.

The Virgin's Miracles

Sure I can imagine Satan being cast out
from someone's mouth,
the possessed breaking free
of chains around his neck and wrists.

But a cure for barrenness—no,
I can't envision that. The loins know better.

As for Her third miracle, I'm still overwhelmed
by that man from Thessaly, brought back from the dead
and simply sailing away.

Raffaello Ceccoli's Icon, 1853

My father liked Ceccoli's icon
because he portrayed his dead daughter
as the Virgin.

I was alive and my father
was not a painter.

"Only this lasts," he'd whisper
as he held me tightly in his arms
like Ceccoli must have held his heavy easel.

But where was the fountain?
In the lion's mouth?
In the churchyard, beyond the tombs?
Deep in the plane trees' shadows?

I wanted that life-giving spring in the open
so the unbroken lifeline of his palm
would always be there,
hidden behind the painting.

Parthenis Visits the Monastery

He paints the fountain and the monks' cells
azure, like Italian farmhouses,
dobs thick foliage over the roofs.

The daughter is rose,
the archangel mauve,
holding a lyre.

As long as the music lasts
the spring will flow,
the lily bloom.

The Well Inside the House

In Toledo, El Greco
once rested his palms against the stone
of a well inside a house
where I once stayed.

Carmen Garcia Márquez,
who owns it now,
once told me that in medieval times
a saint was martyred there.

Her belongings, now stone, are still there.
"Blessed Spring," Carmen calls it,
that well in her inner courtyard
where holy nectar once flowed.

The Source of Her Tears

The source can be a theme,
the woman a theme,
sand and clamshells,
even a hidden vein,
far away from the rolling brook,

humming the song of Fatima Zahra
from Morocco,
the reason for her tears in Sète,
where her love, a flowing spring, has gone.

With one flick of their tails
fish leap high above that spring—
seven fish, alive only
because of her song.

The Experience of Eros

He drinks her in
and feels
the buzzing in her veins

while muzzles
search for the taste of the wild
the shiver—

he drinks her
and she feels
a fountain welling up

snow melts
compressed metals flow

then a shallow pool
and after

the mirage
the perfect consummation—
tongues of narcissi, flowing juices

lost
in themselves.

III.

TRUSTED COLORS

German paint tubes:
Owl 1–12

Chamois paintbrushes and Chinese plates
(wrapped in newsprint soaked in turpentine
to protect them from moths)

Pure linseed oil
(to be tested in one's mouth:
more bitter = more pure)

Turpentine

Belgian canvasses

Portraits with Butterflies

If only you'd get TB and never die. Then I could
pass each morning asking how you are.
—Dirge from Asia Minor

I got consumption
and died at nineteen—
they buried me in the monastery.

*

Take me away from here save me!
Can't you see I've been thrown
off a cliff—
the Black Death.

*

Captured by the Greeks in the Balkan War,
stricken with typhus,
I was forced to help build the Turkish Road,
buried under it.

*

Not on the list
to become a naval officer,
I committed *hara-kiri.* They threw my body
off the Cape.

*

During the Turkish Occupation,
I was executed on the islet of Daskalio.
I was a teacher, they said.

*

Gentlemen, evacuate your houses.
Fire is approaching.

*

Water quick! To put out
the fires from Hell
blackening the leaves
of our lemon trees.

Eleni was right
to plant palms.

*

Black butterflies,
big as a child's hands.

She fondled them,
adorned them.

In the days of August
they evoked for her
something of the Far East.

*

Among the cypresses at the monastery,
the butterflies look like Lilliputians
dressed in black

on their way to the red house
set among the palms. The monks
sense something primal
invading the island.

*

From Hydra,
neither wise nor handsome,
wearing a gold earring,
anxious,
I prefer to hide.

I'm Miltos, the black cat
who walks on waves.
At the White Cat taverna,
where the sandy cove is sinking,
I write postcards to friends.
Cheers!

*

Butterflies, don't go away,
don't leave me
surrounded by blackness. Butterflies,

don't forget me
inside my cousin's black boat.
Or is it Charon's?

Butterflies,
if only you'd devour me.

Devil's Bridge

He paints my eyes
salamander green.

Following his Classical motif, shall I flee
to the Golden River Gorge?

On the bridge, I'm a nymph posing.
Pan, a horned creature,

is pounding his hooves on the rock below
Devil's Rock leaving pawprints.

I'm careful not to slip and fall,
because this bridge
has the Evil Eye—
every thought I project
has to pace back and forth
on that rock below
to stop the beating hooves,
the sunless ungulae of time,
Satan's paws.

Giannis Scarlatos and Xanthoula Kouneli

He started the sketch upside down.
After drawing the broad lines of a sullen face,
he turned it right-side-up and continued.
He made portraits of the royal family,
their nannies with golden braids.
Sitting in the courtyard,
watching him,
I was enraptured.

He was everywhere—
on the news, in the papers.
Leaders of the Levant were all inviting him
to do their portraits—
the Patriarch of Alexandria
and that one with a monocle.

He was a god and she
a wonder of the world—first chair in the National Symphony,
with a scar on her throat from playing the violin.

After his sudden death in Damascus
(though some say Baghdad),
she became a frightened, insecure woman
who wouldn't talk to her brothers and sisters.
She talked to us, though,
and showed us his paintings.
Do you like them? What do you see?

We saw anxious eyes
behind glasses
with butterfly frames.

Distributing the Fruit

Scarlatos makes busts but also
full-length portraits
that allow the body to move inside the frame.
On the face he always leaves adventurous shadings.
He and Kouneli spend summers at the Oasis,
where my father, who has gotten to know him,
gives them pomegranates. Scarlatos
became the great portrait painter
of the Palace and the Greek diaspora.
Even our fruit appear in his paintings.

Giannis Scarlatos's Engagement, 1952

Walking along the beach road,
he stopped at her orchard. She was waiting
among the hundred-leaf roses,
playing strange, cavorting sounds
on her violin.

After she lost him in Baghdad,
she wore a widow's shroud and black gloves,
kept her wedding ring in front of a small bowl
with lemon petals—
a sublime performance.

She closed herself up in the family's seaside house,
where all his portraits interacted
with her coquettish accessories.

Paint Store

For Nikos and Spyros Pavlou

What I liked about our shop was the colors—
Powders, turpentine, linseed oil, desiccants . . .
Going to Piraeus for supplies,
I started learning from a craftsman there.
He had a workshop with a sign in front,
NO ENTRY ALLOWED. I'd go in
to learn the secrets of color.
He taught me about desiccants
and I started looking for the European kind,
not made from resin, the ones they used in icon painting.
From a pharmaceutical warehouse I got
manganese, lead, and other raw material.
"Put them into a brass mortar,"
he told me, "and grind them into powder,
then put 50 drams in a clay pot,
along with half an oka
of pure linseed oil, slowly
mixing it all with a wooden spatula
till everything's blended together.
(At first the mixture is a delicate white,
but with time it yellows, best to cut it
with a bit of blue.)
Then put a few drops of desiccant in a small bottle
and little by little add your color." That's how
I learned my father's work,
by watching and listening.

Our little shop was a haven for the open-minded;
that's why the authorities accused my father
of supporting the Coup of '35. They were putting together

a file in order to have him exiled. The elders
of the local People's Party intervened
and the whole thing was dropped. (People back then
knew how to stand up for each other when it came to politics.)
Georgios Adrianopoulos, the star of Piraeus' football team
joined the People's Party and went into politics.
As soon as he arrived on the island
he came directly to my father's store—
"Nikos, I need your help,"
and because all sorts of people were coming and going
from the shop, my father told everyone,
"Vote bitten for Georgios."

On our island, we weren't using paper ballots
back then. There was a box
for each candidate. If there were five candidates,
there were five boxes. We voted with little gilded balls.
Each box had a "for" side, painted gold,
and an "against" side, painted black. Inside,
the box was divided in two. Once a voter
put his hand inside the hole at the top,
he could choose "for" or "against"
by dropping the ball, without anyone seeing,
into the gold side or the black side.
Zealous voters would show their passion
by biting the lead ball before putting it in.
We called those balls "bitten."

Election officials and supporters of the candidates
would sit in a half-circle around the boxes,

keeping an eye on things. With a slight
flick of his wrist, a voter could show,
without being obvious, who he had voted for.
Sometimes a supporter, when he saw that his candidate
wasn't going to win, would kick over a box,
scattering pellets everywhere, making it impossible
to tell who was winning. That's why, a few years later,
we started using paper ballots.

As for me, I liked movies—
Westerns, histories, swashbucklers.
They were all black and white back then.
Matinées were half-price, 12 drachs.
I'd go to all the cinemas in Athens.

In 1960 I took over the shop.

The Annunciation (1907)

Artists will be persuaded that they must work with mind and soul, not only with paintbrush and chisel.

—Kostis Parthenis

Guardian Archangel,
speak to me of the naked instant
when, from the setting sun
in its ascetic nature,
a sliver of light brought forth
the black between half-closed wings
resting on your shoulders and heels,
and of the girl, the beloved
dressed in a rose-colored gown,
in that instant matter was alchemized,
as if you had already announced it . . .

Kostis Parthenis Rowing

Crossing a watercourse,
a dreamscape,
where trees were steaming,
rearranging themselves,

observer, beholder of fish,
he was watching the refractions.
Why so much silence?

Nervously he grabbed the oars
and rowed full speed
into an urban parlor.

Crimson drapes with heavy brocades,
icons of the Lord . . .
and so he discovered his true sensibility.

The Month of Departures

Georgos Mihail, a shipmaster from Suez,
asked him to frame the Almighty
in gold-leaf.

On the back of the halo
he added,
Papa et mama gratia, addio, pregare per me,
1 Septembre 1907,
il povero Kostis.

He felt weak—
he'd been living on water and dry biscuits
and only now did he try
to go out to the square.

A sea hawk was floating
on currents of air,
getting a feel for the wind.

A fortuitous omen?

Let it be seen as such.

Still Life with No Background

In his last days, Parthenis was cared for
in the Hospital of the Annunciation. Unofficially
we accompanied the funeral procession
one day in July of '67.
He lived in a little ochre house on the Citadel.
Whenever we passed it, our mom would say,
"That's Parthenis' house!"
We learned about him in school.
Mrs. Katina Pappa took us to the Zappeion,
to the First Panhellenic Art Exhibition,
for us to see the *Apotheosis of Athanasios Diakos*,
a painting almost four meters tall and just as wide,
sold to the National Bank for 6,000,000 drachs.
—6,000,000 drachs for a framed piece of canvas?
—We don't say "framed canvas," we say "painting."
—6,000,000 drachs can get an apartment building
on Patission & Spartis if you win
the State Lottery, like that lawyer Iobre.
—And what's an apartment building?
Worthless walls.

The Fateful Summer of Ioannis Kapodistrias, 1831

Nothing is easier
than sinking.
He's afraid of everything.
They deserve it all,
he said to himself.

He thought this would be a time of plenty—
Squares, roads, buildings,
a new school on the island,
a sanatorium, a monastery.

The State will be shipshape
this fall. He was decisive.
The drifting corvette
will find a helmsman.

Then he turned with his big
almond-shaped eyes
toward the naval station—yes,
music from the brass band
was coming in through the open window
like the heavy groan of thunder.

But the light just then
conferred so much charm on the moment.

Like a Midsummer Afternoon

For Athena Papadaki

When she painted us,
her heavily made-up eyes
immersed themselves
in our lives.

We discovered it at her exhibition,
Gianna Paola Cuneo, 2014.
Ethereal women
with heavy jewels,
grieving men from mythology,
that boat with the sail we admired
summer mornings.
                                        And here
my little boy is sunburned
as he looks out at the port
and dreams!

Festival of Dionysos

The breezes on the beach at Galata
were constantly shifting,
but you weren't born yet.

You didn't know, my son, about the games,
how the blacksmiths hammered all winter
to forge the prince, and just as spring arrived,
wrapped him in wire mesh
so we could slip blossoms into the holes
like Legos—

gladiolas, roses, carnations—
you've never seen the beach
crowded with celebrants, floats and marching bands,
how we'd bring chairs down from the houses,
and behold—
a redolent parade!

After three days the body was thrown
into an empty field and we removed
the flowers, tossed them into the sea
as if it were the Ganges,
left that skeleton to rot.
Only his sword, made of carnations,
evoked a hero, and his golden sandals,
first prize for the best float.
What joy!

In your drawings,
you confuse waves
with sky. Winter already,

you play with colored pencils and ask,
do I fly or swim? I can only say,
Make the pageantry
come again, make our road
redolent with flowers.

The Italian Circus on the Moraitiki Shore

Loud music,
all of us applauding—
oh, what a wonder to see Mike Lamar
in top hat, tux and white gloves,
twirling a cane in his hands,
then letting it hover
on its own
in circles around his body.

When the elephant sauntered off
toward the sea, unperturbed,
looking for water, it sank
deep into the sand.
We all gathered around
its huge head
stuck in mud, struggling fiercely.

The performance suspended,
we posed for pictures with the monkeys,

till the circus hands brought ropes
and tied them around the elephant's huge body.

Wailing in desperation,
it kept turning its trunk
round and round in the air,
like Mike Lamar's cane.

Merçi pour le Beau Sejour

For Stavros Deligeorgis

It's so exquisite the road
along the sea at Neorion
this day in September 1952.
Deep sea creatures accompany the painter
as his green hair grows longer and longer.

You sail amid intense color—
not a natural state, you know,
but the light you create
is exactly as the eye,
with its cones and rods,
perceives it.

What you see
is a dream, perhaps that of a young harlequin,
Federico, let's say,
or maybe from your own paintbrush
while fish play a tango with airy movements
on a bandoneon

Olive-Colored Eye
with grey floating specks, Eye
of his lover Bella,
tell me the secret of the acrobats.

—Vermillion and emerald with a touch of black
and spotlights that, like these souls under the Big Top,
know nothing so beautiful as the circus.

The Boat and the Fish

By Marc Chagall (Poros, 1952)

From dry land he sees her
take the form of a fish, a mermaid,
and knows that something about love
is hard and distant.

He's a fisherman and
a man—her motions
there on the tranquil Saronic Gulf
unsettle him. In a little while
the song of lust,

then the plunge:
the boat will touch her,
the fishnet enflame her—

they become
quivering spectrums of the paintbrush,
what the moon brings forth
from its womb.

IV.

WITH A VIEW OF THE SEA

February, the month of departures,
when ships disembark slowly, as in a nightmare.
And everything goes silent.

With a View of the Sea

The steamship KAISER FRANZ JOSEF I
was built in 1911 for the Austrian Union of Trieste
by the Nautical Shipyard in Monfalcone
(Engines from D. Rowan & Co., Glasgow).
Registered gross capacity, 12567 tons.
Length, 477.5 ft.
Width, 60.2 ft.
Two funnels,
two foresails,
double propellers.
Speed, 17 knots.
Capacity, 125 first-class passengers,
550 second-class passengers,
1230 passengers in third-class.
On May 25th, 1912 she embarked on her maiden voyage,
to Trieste, Patras, Palermo, Algeria and New York.
Her last voyage ended on June 13th, 1914.

Group Number:	P00040-4
Page Reference Number:	84
Crew List Page Number:	0014
First Name:	Spyridon
Last Name:	Sakellion
Age:	25 years old
Sex Code:	Male
Marital Status:	Single
Citizen of the U.S.A.:	No
Member of Crew:	No
Nationality:	Hellas, Hellenic
Place of Residence:	Poros, Greece
Name of Ship:	Kaiser Franz Josef I
Date of Arrival:	4th March, 1914
Port of Arrival:	New York
Port of Departure:	Patras
Usual Port of Departure:	Patras, Achaia, Peloponnese.
I.D. Number:	100404100014

I crossed the ocean with its tempests
and massive waves as a passenger in third-class
on the steamship KAISER FRANZ JOSEF I
with many other Greek immigrants,
none from my island.

I stared for hours at the sky of the New World
filled with grey-black veils of smoke.
On Ellis Island they pronounced me completely healthy.
When at dusk we passed
the Statue of Liberty,
I crossed myself,
then tipped my cap to her. So this was New York.
This was America.
This is what I'll be for years,
I said to the seabirds—
an immigrant with a trunk.

I went to America
to make money and buy land
for an orchard back home.
I didn't know the language, though I tried.

This is a face.
The eyes, nose, and mouth
are parts of the face.

I would send money home
from McCallie Avenue, Chattanooga, Tennessee,
all in my father's name.
When I returned to the island,
the money was gone.

I joined the army,
volunteered for the Balkan Wars,
volunteered for the Great War as well.
On the battlefield, I was infantry.
With my trusty rifle and the help of God,
I survived that burning hell,
though I did start smoking.

This is the body.
The head. The arms. The legs.
These are a man's parts.

Back in the New World,
I didn't wander about.
I became a restauranteur.
I stayed in one place, became a ghost.
No one could see me
to save me.

Ten years passed.
Swelling waves kept pounding my door.
Suddenly, my partner and I
made a fateful decision—
we burned down the restaurant
to split the insurance.

In that Southern state
that would soon expel me,
I saw the greedy fire swallowing up
the wrought-iron tables, our dishes, and silverware.
Inside those dancing flames

I saw my island
tongues of fire caressing its mountains.
At that moment I wanted nothing more
than to plant some trees,
see the fruit they'd bear.

Closed up in those trees,
he saw houses with doors and windows
floating by. The sea was not on fire.
He went silent.

Back home, my sisters were becoming
heavy and impatient. I filled a Bayonne
with their dowry and a carpet
depicting Armistice Day. On the ship
I stood at the gunwale day and night,
a cigarette in my mouth,
eager to see the port of Patras.
Lord, take the salt from my eyes.

On the island, I found my relatives
changed, with many children.
For weeks I observed the mills
on the ridges of hills,
the mechanical clock with a chime like a bell,
sailors marching and playing trumpets.
Glory be to God.

Finally I bought an orchard,
became a landowner.
I loved that plot of land;
loved the earth,
the way it blossomed in spring;

loved the chickens pecking at it,
the dogs protecting it,
the cistern collecting rainwater,
the draw-wheel, hoist and vertical gears,
the horse treading around in circles.
I even loved the ditches I irrigated,
could find them with my eyes closed.
High time to find a wife.

Before our wedding, Nina worked at home,
making hats with fabrics she'd buy from Ermou
in Athens. All the officers' wives
wanted to wear her hats at the big receptions,
whatever matched their coats and gowns.
They'd come for a fitting
since she had all the latest patterns,
would do every correction they asked.

A hat has angles and curves, a pose.
It hides the brow with great care,
with a veil or black satin spangles,
or a brim sometimes
angled above an eye
for a touch of the erotic.

They wanted to marry her off
to a pharmacist,
a marine officer,
men with a bright future. In the end,
she chose a man with a past
and stopped making hats.

"I was born in Bulgaria" she told me,

"beside the Danube. They named me Irene.
My father, a barge captain, would ply his boat
back and forth across the river." At the wedding
Ponirakis, who owns nurseries,
was our best man. He planted calla lilies and tulips
for us, red grapes beside the cistern,
and asphodels. Our land became a flourishing garden.
We had two strong children.
I baptized them at the monastery,
gave them both durable names.

They were born
in the time of large investments—
his faith in the future was restored.

The tongues of leaves tell me
inside the earth there's a plan inscribed.
I imagine a network of roots
that thrive there, elusive and unbaptized.
She whispers to me,
"The trees are holding back,"
and I look for changes
in our citrus fruit:

time here is dense and abrupt,
there, underground it spirals up in tranquility.

This is a stem.
This is a pot.
This is the cover for a pot.
This is a flame.

*

When the Germans came, we couldn't make money
from the orchards, but we had the restaurant where Nina
used as many lemons as she could,
gave her recipes to cousins:

Lemon Blossom Spoon-Sweet

100 drams of well-chosen blossoms.
1 oka of sugar.

Put water on to boil
and add the blossoms.
Boil them 4–5 times,
then drain the water,
put in fresh water
and boil the blossoms again
until you can tell with your fingers,
like we test greens,
that they're thoroughly boiled.
Once ready, prepare a bowl of lemon juice,
pour it over the mixture and leave it in the sun
for an hour. Later dilute it with 5–6 cups of water.
Add the sugar, stirring it carefully until
the lumps are gone,
then lower the flame as much as possible,
letting it simmer slowly, so it doesn't turn black.

PS Dear Semiramis, Give your kids a kiss for me!

*

Taverna on a sidestreet with bakeries:
Picarel
Retsina from Foussa
Touloumi Cheese with Must

Our restaurant was on a sidestreet
that opened out to the square.
My son was a helper. During the war
he rode a horse
and would go to Damala,
the village across the strait from us.
We'd throw a brown blanket over the trees
so he knew it was safe to return.
If he didn't see it, he'd go back. One day
my wife forgot to remove the blanket,
so he set off. "Halt!" the Germans shouted.
Was he the one who's been hiding weapons,
gasoline, and diesel inside a well?
He ran away with all his might.
As he was jumping off a drystone wall
into a field, they shot at him.
A bullet grazed his ear. They caught him,
searched him, found a dictionary.
Full of blood, he was taken to be executed
in the square. I ran to the collaborator,
promised to give him my land,
the family home, all the olive oil, everything
if he could save the boy.
"He's not responsible.
He's just learning English. He likes
foreign languages."

Look, a pocket-book:
What is this?
This is an animal.
These are more animals: a goat, a pig, a horse.
What is this? This? THIS?—

Still trying to save the boy
I ran to my neighbor Matina,
who spoke German, begged her to go to the soldiers
and explain. She returned an hour later with the boy.

*

The bay was receding more and more.
The boats had their sails pulled in.
Frantically he was crossing the waterfront
as if flames were licking at his feet;
the horses were whinnying, waves spewing up,
the fishing boats whistling in the wind,
a window banging—her wailing
filled the side streets
like a siren.
Who decides survival?

Ice is solid.
This is ice.

The cypress trees suddenly leaned over the house
as Nina said to her son, I'm falling.
For nights, an acrobat, she'd been falling,
the sea, full of rocks, receding,
and she couldn't swim. When she recovered,
everyone needed something, each making demands
in a different tone of voice.

*

I told my son he had to become an agronomist.

He refused,
so I threw him out of the house,
slammed the door behind him.
By 1955 we had reconciled
and he was selling our lemons.

These are lemons.
These are oranges.
Lemons and oranges are fruit.

Ours was the only region that produced really good lemons,
four times per year, sometimes twice in the summer.
They were selling for 2 drachs a crate
(before the war they were sold by the crate,
not by weight). We made a good income.

Workers from Poros loaded the local boats
that went to Odessa. With a “Heave to!” and a “Strike sail!”
the boats would dock and unload—
bricks, black caviar, and Russian wheat.
They’d sail all over to the Black Sea, the Adriatic,
Constantinople, Constanța in Romania,
Burgas in Bulgaria, Trieste, Venice, Bari, Ancona.
The sea had killed many. The boats that got home first
took the best prices. All the boats
had top-notch captains. Exposed to the wind and rain,
our sailors wore rain-slicks treated with linseed oil
and black paint. They kept good care of them
so they’d last for years. Later, in the time of Dengue fever,
we built wheelhouses,
planted lemon trees everywhere.
Some bore fruit seven times a year.

A gram of lemon juice was good as a disinfectant.
Golden trees, we called them. They cured everything.

They loaded the crates onto the fishing boats one by one,
not all together, because when one crate went bad
it would become a whole pillar of rot.
In summer they took out their stoves and whitened
the green lemons so they could sell them
in Volos, Thessaloniki, Kavala, Mount Athos.
The heat bleached them, made them look like good lemons,
though this was considered cheating.

*

In November of 1955, Panagiotis, my former partner
who, in America, married my cousin Marousso
and fathered six healthy children,
came to the island to see me. I brought out
a demijohn of wine from a bottom shelf
and we drank the whole night,
remembering how, all our lives
we've been living at the edge of a cliff,
remembering too the fire we started. We laughed and laughed.
Coughing hard all the next day, my insides torn up,
I filled a basin with spit and blood.
Everyone thought it was wine.

*

A boat angles toward the purple sunset
and in a calm place far away

I see the trees in the big parks,
the cannon on the hilltop,
roll a cigarette,
and gaze into her eyes
as my last breath wraps around her
like a shroud.

The house is draped, inside and out, in black—
his lanky body fills the dining room,
and she, who knew she loved him,
knew they would always be happy together,
is slamming the chairs loudly,
stomping the floorboards. Just then
an intangible enormity sails free
from his dead body,
passing into the rhythm of the sea.

Air comes in.
                                        Goes out.
That's a breath.

In   out
            one breath

in   out
            two breaths

in   out

in   out   out   out

V.

THE PALACES

Field guide to death
(October 12, 323 BC):

Genus: Hemlock, the Spotted Poison
(*Conium maculatum*)

Family: Skiadofora
(*Umbelliferae*)

The Palaces

I'd been studying my death for a long time.
Spread out, it cast a shadow over me.
Here, in this steadfast sanctuary,
is where I belonged.

But, in my mind, I was never really here.
This was the island of Apollo,
Poseidon,
and the revered dead.
For a split second
they overlapped.
That's when I could have escaped.

The soldiers would've been deeply tormented.
Archias' stern officer's face
might've gone wet with remorse.
The smoke would've ascended smoothly,
turning the leaves over
in first light.

Instead of dedicating myself to my city,
I live freely among the pines here,
where, just as all narratives
end with some message,
this forest has meaning.
Night is falling.
From the depths of the sea
I arrive under their foliage.

Help him to forget,
Poseidon, father of everything,
help him . . . .

The Macedonians are still rowing through the night.
I, my dearest Poseidon
(calling from salt-white sails and riggings),
still live amazed by this temple.
Antipatros and all the Macedonians
have not left your temple unpolluted.
For ages I could touch the massive stones
and gaze at the fugitives
arriving at the shrine,
pouring out their libations.

A traveler found the path through the pine forest
and guided me to this white temple.
My bones were buried beneath the monastery,
in the company of priests,
while I wandered mumbling bitter,
hateful words, until she with the consumptive body
strode over me, calmed me
with prayers in an alien tongue,
so showed me the way
back to this place
where time nurtures the hemlock,
that leafy herb.

Temple of the Trident, 1976

Following the protocol
of farewell, you waited,
Demosthenes.

I see the swords,
the gleaming shields,
the snakelike path to change
on the hard shins.

Nowhere on the horizon is there a straight line.

—What I wanted
was an answer to your question.
—My question?
    —"Where did I find the strength?"

Vagionia Delta

I was searching by the sea
for the ancient harbor. Did an earthquake
destroy it? Alaric and his Visigoths?

I was searching for the words
of the ancient storytellers—
Whatever leaves is lost.

It was a small cove,
an open domicile of rocks,
the keels shining, the sea
tearing itself apart.

Temple of Poseidon, 1965

In the morning when excursions to the temple take place,
the children run among the olive trees and pines,

while grasshoppers with diaphanous wings
form circles in the dirt.

Someone is playing a mandolin
as we get drunk on ouzo.

He told you he'll take you, so *why not marry?*
He told you he'll marry you, you've never been matched.

Our youth is going, our beauty; they won't ever return.
Our youth is going, our beauty, never again to return.

Kammeni Peak sticks out its lava tongue
and soon silver wedges of islands rise from the sea—

Petrokaravo, Angistri, Aegina,
Moni, Plateia, San Giorgio.

From high above, the waves seem stationary—
a serpent has numbed them.

According to testimonials from that time,
after the litany ended
the cloud of locusts
would disappear into the sea.
For this event
Saint Tryfonas always had the proper exorcism.

The God

He conjured up
two or three islands,
barren and craggy,
to guard it.

A small universe
with the feverish
spirit of the night.

Shades of Algerians
and Illyrians.

The cold breeze
like a web to cover us.

Vigil

The night of the temple sacrifice
emerged from the sifting screen:

Lamps had been lit for the last banquet.
The usual animals for the sacrifice—
pigs, lambs, and calves.

Some parts of the carcass
were given to the priest, some
to the god.

I notice a shard
of the sacrificial knife
in a woman's hand.

But what are these children
doing at the sacrifice?
Among the broaches and spears, axes and weights
why are these statues of children
here?

And who was wearing this ring
with a gold-black heron?

Let's go look for it. Let's go.

Recording the Sacrifices

Each day the animals chosen
for the sacrifice
were recorded—
cost, age, and quality,
the type of wood used,
which fatlings for the children.

*

Until 1979, at the site of the sanctuary,
there was a farmhouse and a stable
that belonged to the sap collectors—
a good income. They came to the island
from Angistri
in the early twentieth century.

They would hack at the pine trunk and insert a triangular funnel
to collect the resin—in earlier times they'd pound with a rock
until the sap started dripping. Later they'd collect the sap
in a pit and add some wine.
The sap soaked up as much as it wanted.

*

Barefoot since childhood,
Nota showed her friend
how she found Poseidon's marble foot—
why wouldn't the old god
want to chase her?

She grew chubby, with thick, bushy hair.
We called her Big-Butt.
She fell in love with a young man from Brinia.
Her father wouldn't consent
because he had a grudge against the guy.

The girl grew melancholy,
slowly went crazy.
To avoid gossip, her six siblings
left her at the Temple of Poseidon,
her family coming and going.

We called the father Kemal.
One day, while he was sleeping
wrapped in a blanket,
the daughter grabbed a hoe,
pounded his head over and over,
replaced the blanket and left.

Her mother, returning from church that Sunday,
saw him lying there. "Wake up,"
she told him, "Why won't you wake up?"
He didn't budge. Pulling the blanket
away, she screamed
and went looking for her daughter.

My father, who kept pigs,
went to open a spigot so the animals could drink.
Meeting the girl on the road, he said,
"Good morning." No answer.

She’s lost to the winds, he thought to himself,
doesn’t even say good morning.
Her mother went to her friend Evanthia,
never said a word about anything.

Nota died in the psychiatric hospital.
I would visit her until the end.
She was calm, soft-spoken.
The seamstress married her beau.
My sisters-in-law would have their dresses sewn there.
All the siblings suffered many misfortunes.
Her favorite brother died in a shipwreck
on his way to Alaska.

Only children born on Saturday
see the light in her farmhouse.
She sees the beautiful clothes,
the wedding table in the Palaces,
her girlfriends with her black knight.

Like the Hamsin, you ravaged my desolate soul
and now I’m burning, burning, burning.

You enslaved me, maimed me, and now I want to die
to have, in the underworld,
my pierced heart for company
while lusting madly
for the upper world I love.

Demosthenes the Athenian on Kalavria

Craftsmen restored the statues
in the Temple of Heroes
along with the railings and small pillars,
riveted the eagle back in place,
including its tail-feathers and broken beak,
and finally, with a pantograph, made a bust
of Demosthenes, the famous orator.

The one we still have,
the one we cope with.
The head has come unglued several times.
Drunks threw stones at it during the Metaxas dictatorship.
Naturally the perpetrators were imprisoned,
the bust reglued. But the adhesive
still keeps coming loose. By now,
from the bust's many falls, the nose
and part of the neck have broken off.

Remember: islanders go tame,
highlanders grow wild.

Originally made with marble from Dionysos,
a gift to the town from Rear Admiral Khatziloukas,
it's now held in place by volcanic rock.
The orator looks out on the path
to the Monastery and Fousa, where,
in the shadows, hemlock flares up.

V.

HANDIWORK OF UNIQUE VALUE

Vigil Candle:

one glass of water,

two fingers of olive oil,

a wick made from horehound

found in the surrounding mountains

Galini—His Last Strait

Take it, I give it to you.
See, it's a lily pad.

*

Now, what house is this?
The water lilies in the cistern
so close, so close to the sea,
and so much sand,
so many names.
The villa has a staircase,
an oil lamp. The owner's arrival
depends on who calls.

No visitors today.
The lady of the house is resting.
The lady of the house is worried.
The lady has her daughters with her,
going up and down the staircase,
tossing clothes here and there.

No, today we are at home,
with our iron bed,
our meager furniture.

*

The poet's bedroom looks out on a field.
He listens to the frogs in the cistern.

In the morning he will contemplate the broken masts
of the sunken mail ship, the Thrush,
and hear the hiss of poisonous snakes.
Leisurely he will swim out
to the island of the teacher—
free-style, crawl, backstroke, butterfly.
His biceps resemble a lumberjack's,
his calves a hoplite's.

*

It's not time, not time yet
to wed.
She sticks her tongue out and you laugh.
She strips her clothes off, smiles
and enters, there, where your life,
the life of a frog-prince
on a water lily, changes—
So, let go of this house,
the house by the sea,
the house of the spirits

*

He said to Maro, "Hold on.
The pine needles in the sand are slippery,
hold on to me."

His afternoon is quiet.
The passing light is golden.
He's been cutting wood for the fireplace.

Now he stands at the big
stained-glass window
while on the hall ceiling
a dark ship is multiplying.
He ascends to it with her,
gently raising the mask of the coastline—

Galini, with what playful rhythm
do you define the fullness of life?
A one and a two and a one two . . .

Suddenly
all the frogs go quiet.

Guestbook

A sailor in his summer uniform,
hibiscus flowers,
the purple mountain—
drawings in the guestbook depicting summer.
Many had visited. We too passed by outside.

“They made movies here.”
“Venizelos once came to visit.”

The foundation stone was laid on January 12, 1894.
While digging, they found two capitals,
a grave with bones,
an ancient clay pot.
Some said a leper colony. Others a graveyard.

*

Let’s be precise, Maro.
Did you mean Coriolano or Cormorant?

Close the shutters.
Is it getting hot or is my fever rising?

It’s difficult raising children.
You were always reserved.

Near the sea one forgets everything.
Everything. Will you depart by ship?

Now, do you have the courage
to count the number of people you’ve loved?

I can't stop the light.
Will you remember us, Antigone?

Cyclamen Graecum

In August of '36 he said to my mother,
"Come to the war as my wife."
The iron door opened.
The iron pushed hard.
She left with him.

Telegrams followed—
twenty words at most,
perhaps a letter with photographs.
Adventure, Emotion, Anxiety,
in part about "The Thrush," in part the "White Horse,"
in part her, in part the king.

He painted mermaids with twin tails
tied, like her blonde braids,
in a knot over their heads,
and wrote in a poem,
"Take the child with you,"
But, but . . . .

In the fall, the mountain behind Galini
is covered in wild cyclamen.
He'd gather bouquets
and offer them—
by now, for me, they only mean
good-bye.

Ghost in Black & White

Though the photo is faded,
his Royal Navy uniform
still suits him,
a shirt with dark stripes,
a pleated scarf
tucked under the big collar,
and on his head
a cap with the name of his ship.

It's the only picture I have, the official one.
Isn't he photogenic?
The painted rocks and clouds
are an appropriate backdrop,
but not the weapon he's holding.

Each time he cocks it,
he blinks.

Coat of Arms

For Nellie Kyriakaki and Dimitris Grivas

My father loved me a lot.
They took him into the Navy because
of our family's standing.
His aunts lived on Hydra.
One was engaged to some guy
who'd bring them chests filled with gifts from Russia.
When I'd visit, they'd give me costume jewelry—
gold rings, a cross made from mother-of-pearl.
They had land in Kokkinia, so many lemon trees
they'd rent them out to nearby farmers.

In '33, when my mother died from heart failure,
father had to send me to the French nuns
at Joan of Arc School, on Filonos in Piraeus.
I ate my meals there, but lived with my cousins
in a house he rented on Karaiskou, near the Municipal Theater.
He said to my aunt, "I want you to love her
for me. She won't be a burden,"
and whispered in my ear
"If by chance you end up living alone,
your aunt will look after you."

Nina took me everywhere.
She'd come to Piraeus just to see me.
She'd talk about a lot of things,
encouraged me to take up dancing—
tango, foxtrot, waltz. All the officers
with their striped uniforms danced them.
Some evenings she'd hum me to sleep:

Oh mon Dieu de Paris, donne-moi un mari
pour passer avec lui une bonne nuit.
My dreams at night were always good.

After a year or so we moved to Athens—
into a big house with a yard facing the road.
I started to go to a different school, Saint Joseph's.
When I grew up, I wound up using my French
in my husband's retail store.
I loved the language.

Lessons for the Poros Naval Base

For Angeliki Sidira

"With his middle and index fingers on her waist,"
my father taught me, "the hilt of his sword between them,
the man holds the lady at a distance,
while his right hand finds your left. This is the way,
according to Navy protocol,
you waltz at the balls, my dear,
and do Russian quadrilles."

We'd dress up in furs and they
in their formal whites, swords at their sides.
The older ones would play rummy,
squandering all their money
to Perry Como and Pat Boone,
drums and trumpets,
whiskey, vermouth and rock & roll,
foxtrots, sambas, hesitations and rumbas
and, at the end Venetian barcarolles.
Later, a moonlight swim.

At Easter, Father Procopius,
who disclosed my confessions to my father,
would call out at the end of the midnight service,
"Open the Gates!"
And after, in the Palace,
with its high-ceilinged hall and heavy drapes—
velvet chairs around an enormous banquet table.

The Return

He wanted to hear lemurs
singing to him at night,
like whales.

Where to find a lemur here?

A sailor brought him a monkey from Asia.
He played in the garden like a cat,
and when we whitewashed the wall,
he peed all over it.

Father got sick
and the monkey grew melancholy.
When we tried to feed him, he'd raise his paw
and flip us off.

They died one month apart.
Father first.

Matina and the Story of Extermination

Matina Kouneli knew German,
so they took her to their headquarters
as an interpreter. When she learned
that someone was about to be arrested,
she'd tell him to leave immediately,
"You're in danger."

The father of one of the men she had saved
denounced her. The Germans arrested her,
kept her with the prisoners waiting to be executed.
Nearby there were other prisoners
about to go to the camps. She heard them
and managed to sneak into their cell,
like a small, cowardly rabbit.

Later, she'd recount the endless journey by train.
Eighteen months at Auschwitz.
Mengele using her as a lab animal,
filling her body with hormones.
How, when the camps were liberated,
they all descended the Death Stairs, free.

My father was an agent at the Fifth Customs House
in Piraeus. In memory of Matina,
he let the survivors pass without inspecting them.
One day he told us:

"In the customs house, looking at those returning,
my soul wallowing in grief from what I was seeing,
I felt someone fall on me, hugging me hard

and shouting, 'Uncle, Uncle!' Then I saw her—
two huge eyes and enormous breasts
on a skeleton."

From Matina's camp, only three Greek women survived.
In 1981 the German government
sent them compensation.
The women returned it with a note:
"Use the money to console
those who feel guilty."

Matina loved Leonardo.
Every morning they put on flippers and masks
and went spearfishing for octopus.
They'd pass by us looking like large fish
flapping gracefully on the surface of the water.

She'd dance a lot and sing at Sotiris' taverna
in the evening. Her right hand was paralyzed
by radiation; she couldn't play the accordion
like she used to so played with just one hand.

When she died, Leonardo,
who had a heart condition,
stopped taking his medication.

One summer two German women came asking for her.
Oh, dear child,
let us be your joy
now and for all eternity.
Su se su su su sclaf mein Kindelein.

The Magical LP 412

For my brother

Our boat didn't stay in the sea year-round.
In June, before we'd launch her,
we had to submerge her to expand the joints.
Then, with small buckets, we'd bail out
several cubic meters of water,
fore and aft.

We'd scrub the benches and the bulkheads,
the smell of gas and wet wood wafting around us.

Built in Spetses,
LP 412 wasn't made for rowing, which is why,
every year, we struggled hard at the oars.
We named her *Joy.*

Canal

Naval engineers
opened the shallow channel
across a wide spit of sand.

We'd turn the engine off
and lie back clumsily
as the channel widened.

Imagine how this spit of land was once
part of the mainland opposite.
The earth nearby trembled and shook.

Following the canal,
we'd watch the ducks on the banks,
careful not to hit our heads on the low bridge.

If you put your ear to the indentation
in the middle of the bridge,
you can hear weeping and wailing.

The Yard

For Thanos Sakelliou

The little shed on our property smelled of grease,
like a machine shop, and fish. The iron door
would get stuck, so you'd have to push hard
to get in. There were gaffs inside,
nets and fishing lines,
all my father's equipment and tools.

In the yard, he'd untangle the lines
salt the prawns,
store them overnight
in our old IZOLA,
the one he bought when I was born.

What Glistened

Every morning at the beach
I'd gather crabs for bait.
The bottom of the sea
was full of black algae
like drowned hair. I was afraid
to put my feet into all that hair—
eels or earwigs might bite me.

Shiny seahorses
floated up from the bottom,
small-winged and proud,
and shrimp,
almost transparent
in all that blue.

Now, the sea has changed.
They've all been lost.

Body in the Light

Descending to the seabed,
he saw it lying there, immobile
in the refracted light and sand,
opening and closing its mouth—

a Southern Stingray,
20–25 kilos.

He brought it to us,
its belly bloated
with the body of a seagull
it had swallowed.

Living in Silver

There were pikes in the water around Modi.
It takes big hooks and real skill to catch them.

In the morning my father
would gather garfish for bait,
pass a line through each one's belly,
pull it out through the mouth.

One day, in the crevice of a rock,
archaeologists found a pewter box
crusted with plankton,
and inside, the skeleton of a baby
surrounded by cruets and mirrors.

No shells. No beads.
Instead of baubles and toys, the waves
gave her leaden joints.

Watching them work, my father told me
"That Mycenaean mother must have felt
her baby's bones would be protected there."

From that time on, I was constantly close by
while he was fishing. He assumed I belonged with him.

"The sea is the cure for everything," he'd say.
It became my refuge too.

I'd catch octopus,
troll for bait.

Menses and the Sea

Swimming in the sea was the high point of our day.

Because of this, without us knowing, a really private matter would get around. “She’s not swimming today. She’s got the curse,” one adult would say to another, winking. So all the grownups learned when we had our time of the month. And the boys sensed how vulnerable we were to the weather, how easily we’d catch cold from the sea, how much our bellies hurt.

Shut indoors, caught up in this little secret, we played board games pretended to be miserable, while outside, that other sea swept away the secrets of the bathers.

The Slaughterhouses

On days we took the boat to go buy shrimp and fish for red snapper, we'd let the engine idle as we approached the slaughterhouses, passing the skiffs with calves tied by their horns to the oarlocks.

Boatmen hurled the calves up to the stone houses, where workers stabbed them in the nape with a small-blade knife, then slit their throats.

The channel would fill with blood, Punta turn red, Stavrós beyond.

Dangling from hooks, with a suffocating stench, calf-heads swung to and fro in the breeze.

Sneaking a look back, we could see, sometimes, packs of dogfish.

Tselevinia

The sun on his knees,
his thighs, his head,
her father was moving
in slow circles
around the boat.

Come closer, so we can meet,
Beast. Welcome.
I classify you at last
out of existence!

"The currents are strong here!
Be careful, Father, the sharks are coming!
And they're looking for blood!"

Pentimento

The sun’s high up
and still he’s waiting,
raising his hand into the air
to his own rhythm,
so the fish will come,
find the bait
one hundred meters down
in the icy darkness
and take it,
so he can feel
on his line
that sudden pull.

Watery Miracle

In the Bogazi Strait
the sea was calm,
but in one place
water spewed up
like a fountain
in slow motion,
bubbles gushing.

At first, she was here on the surface,
later, farther down,
later still, she disappeared completely.

Suddenly she revealed herself
upright on the prow of his boat.

He took a while to return.
As he docked
he was whispering to himself
The boat smells of incense.

Initiation

When he’d sink his trident to the bottom,
I could hear the sound of his breathing
in the bay of Askeli.

One day, suddenly,
the wind picked up the prow of our boat
and we found ourselves in the eye of a sirocco.

He dove to the depths and rose
like a flayed boulder.

In the iridescence of the water,
timeworn storm lamps,
the face of the sea god.

The Gate

All night beside him
in the endless glow
of his fishing lamp,
I dole out sand and oil
in a cove where the Sleeping Woman
disappears.

"Give me your hand, my child," he says,
"The signs for the weather are auspicious."
But I set my course
by the scops owl,
which is infallible and blunt
and doesn't budge.

Descent into Hades

I listen closely to the stories of the others.
Around us desolation.
Time is ours at last.

The cypresses darken.
The birds go silent.
I watch the fish splashing in the bay.

Father's shade
shows me the eggs they jettison,
the seashells with their luminous inhabitants.

As the shore recedes,
the bones of the souls light up.

Soirées Musicales

For Anna Papazafeiropoulou

I was learning to adapt my fingers
to the darkness—
they were the black keys, and the white
were the light.

In all the maritime provinces,
the houses had a piano.

Anna was playing
and I was looking outside
at the fountain with the dolphins.

Marine Education at the Beginning of the Twentieth Century

In this wooden hut
I am putting on
a one-piece bathing-suit
and a cap. Mornings,

I swim for hours.
The algae kiss the starfish
and curl up,

while the urchins
without moving
kiss me,

exciting me all over
with the words they whisper
to my flesh.

Nearby—
small willows, eucalyptuses,
and a dock for my lover
to berth his boat.

Greta Garbo at Kyveleia

> *My family was poor. I started working at 14, in a beauty parlor. Then fate came along in the guise of director Mauritz Stiller.*
> —Vasilis Koutouzis, in an interview

For Georgos and Katerina Antoniou

We didn't know her,
but the Athenian holiday-makers
kept turning to look at her.
In a pastry-shop on the waterfront
she was the only blonde.

I liked the huskiness of her voice,
how she tittered when she laughed,
putting a hand over her lips,
and the way, while enjoying her sweet,
she stretched her calves and straightened her skirt.

We were teenage boys in the boondocks,
savoring a sweet and watching her.
I decided, then and there:

I'd marry a blonde who smokes
and has arched eyebrows,
and become a hairstylist.
In my own salon,
above the mirror,
I'd hang a portrait of her.

The Link with My Body

For Xanthoula Kouneli-Paloglou

Every year when we arrived at Askeli,
my father treated me like a boy.
He'd lock up my shoes
so I had to go around barefoot.
Stepping in dirt made me feel powerful.
When he was working in the orchard,
which was always in disarray,
he'd whistle for me to come help.

One day, I heard him whistle,
came running and stepped on a nail
jutting from a piece of wood. "Quick,"
he said, "run into the sea and squeeze it
hard, so lots of blood comes out,
then get back fast.
We have work to do."

I suffered a lot back then.
But I became who I am—
tough as nails.

I owe that to Askeli.

The Vegetable Gardens

We'd all draw water from the well—

Efstathiou, Karadima, Kouneli,
Rodi, Sakelliou, Tzanou,
Chrisanthopoulou, Makri—

and pour it into the cistern
to irrigate the gardens.

Then the tadpoles would lose their way.

We'd poke at them in the mud
to make them wiggle.

The Geometry of Stone

The well beneath the arches
was our church—
wide, with a big reservoir
built shallow on purpose
so its water wouldn't reach the sea.
How eels got inside
we could never figure out.

The mason who built it would tell us,
"Such wells are expensive to build.
No other like it on the island.
I call it 'The Font of Siloam,'
an unsung jewel.

Hewn by hand, its stones
from the middle to the top
are andesite, and below,
local stones
of a different base metal—
denser, more solid, they'll never
absorb water. With time,
they tighten.

Can you see its central vault?
No way that guy's gonna fall."

Love Harbor

It’s true. My grandmother told me.
John Lennon himself showed up
at her front door one night in November,
not long before he was killed
across from Central Park. He was scared
and came to Love Harbor
so she could throw the Tarot for him.

“I’m Stella, Mina. Stella,
and I have with me my great good friend.”

She put the axe aside, opened the door
and offered them both hot tea.

“I feel nightmares closing in on me,”
he told her, “something very evil.”

She laid the cards out on the table,
a second time, a third,

and felt her soul darken more and more.
He listened pensively.

They left in the middle of the night,
yet another night like now.
They couldn’t stay any longer.

How strange, another night like this one—
early winter, before the bullet
enters the realm of fulfillment.

Tectonics

For Dionysis Pavlou

Beer, Peppermint, Cointreau, Cognac, Cherry Liqueur—
serve what you want, construct
as many hotels, pensions, and apartments blocks
as you can. No tourist will come here.
Askeli is too old and run down.

Though the government's collapsing,
they've approved a redevelopment plan—
a leisure park with playgrounds,
a promenade fronting the sea.

Now protests, public meetings, posters everywhere—
the signatures must be revoked!

Short History of a Deluge

The river with turtles and lichen
filled with rubble last winter,
carried it all down to the sea,
where it clogged up the seaside with debris.
The ravine continued to fill
with rocks and sediment,
all that rubble uprooting huge pines,
dumping them into the sea as well.
With all that silt and detritus,
the sea changed color.

We didn't notice
till it flooded the asphalt,
surrounded our houses with crabs,
and covered the road with fish.

"If only a sirocco would come,
even a small one,"
some said, and others,
"Will the sea ever recover?"

Bird of Death, April 21, 1967

Everyone remembers exactly where
they were when they heard the news.

Did the recess bell ring?
Did my mother pick me up early?
Did I run down the stairs?
Did the teachers speak of revolution,
say it's all so sudden?

I associated it with Alas, with Callas,
with prizes I found in packs of Klein—

While the tanks were bruising Acharnon Street
and Mt. Parnitha was slowly disappearing beyond the horizon,
while the other side appeared strung upside down
behind the image of a dark soldier
with the phoenix rising from a burning nest,

I learned to watch newsreels,
to follow the parades,
the bucolic life that began
with the same musical passage.

To celebrate football fanatically—

One goal, two goals, Pantso
high in the air—
Hellas is rising up;
One goal, two goals, what a day,
spring is forever in the heart.

To keep distances and make minute distinctions.
To hide behind walls that weren't there.

To make tight braids
and enjoy the boys' crewcuts.

I learned to speak official Greek,
to conjure up spells and riddles (always a student),
smile oblivious
to everything happening around me.

The Conquest, July 21, 1969

After the moon-landing I thought I could walk on water
and balance myself like Armstrong.
With an expression of maximum intensity,

aunt Voula fixed *loukoumades* in the kitchen,
all of us, sweet and ecstatic, shouting, “Yippee!”
looking first at the moon, then at the black & white image
on TV—it too
had scales and grey holes at dusk.

“Ah, those Americans,” she said,
“first *Peyton Place* then the moon!”

As for me, I didn’t know
where I wanted to travel first,
to the moon
or to America.

Since Childhood

Think of the body on the sand,
palms and arms open wide—
an arrow cleaving the air,
a brief surprise in the heavens
before it changes course
and falls to the earth
where it belongs,
and in the process
making a bridge.

Think of the neck and chest extended,
the waist and pelvis straining,
the pull of every tissue,
the practiced body in an earthly arc
just to add another color,
the one that over the years
we forget.

The indelible one.

Cadenza

The director would set up the empty chairs,
one next to the other, their backs against the wall,
each with a view of the sea,
not only the August sea, but also
the opposing knoll of Spheria Island
and Aderes, the huge mountain changing colors
with the seasons,
lights multiplying in the course of time,
the Bay of Askeli remaining landlocked.

The basic structure: family and friends.
Alternating characters narrate conversations
that happened in that same place
by people who have passed away.
A neighbor passes by, says good evening,
presents his news and leaves. Later his narration
becomes a part of the dialogue,
its rhythm,
their sense of community.

Eros and Thanatos, as She Felt It

Kalavria, 1949

Mother is dying.
Her doctor suggests a house by the sea,
with curtains opening and closing in the breeze.
That way, if someone gallops by
under the lemon trees,
her pillow will smell of green twigs.

Call it luck, fate, destiny, fortune, karma, kismet,
whatever you want—
we found his old house.

My threads embroidered his body.
We married.

Film of an Engagement Party in a Lemon Orchard

April 21, 1952

Wave, stop time
so she can live the scenes again
before the hourglass begins.
The boat with the guests is docking—
the godfather of the story, from Constantinople,
has the dark eyes of a photographer.
Photo Lumière, his shop, is in Beyoglou.

Now, in Ophelia's dress,
she's in the eye of the camera,
lemon blossoms in her hair.
A curl falls to the forehead
of the groom with his shining gaze.
He touches her and light explodes.

The evening primroses haven't opened yet.
The guests raise their glasses,
make the gestures of a spell.
In slow motion, he embraces her,
whispers in her ear and so
repels death.

In the cistern, water quietly laps,
creating the illusion of a colonnade
where an ancient eel and tadpoles slide by.
Beyond the unused pumps,
the low hanging lemons
entice us all.

As the clean skin of the film
is inscribed on the wall
and in the hourglass
sparkling sand begins to shift,

from your side of the orchard,
take a breath, listen
to the dense rustle of the lemon trees,
and grasp, my Love, the soul's ritual.

Tree of Life

When I was young my mother had an operation. What remained was a scar crossing her back like a swollen rivulet, and a small, transparent box inside of which was a tiny tree, porous and grey, with many branches—what the doctors uprooted from her damaged kidney and gave to her, in that box, like a present. She placed it carefully inside her drawer.

My mother's name is Zoe, which in Greek means "Life," so I called it "Tree of My Life." Later, in the East, I found carpets with the Tree of Life woven into them. This one was an apple tree, with round, red fruit. Under its thick foliage, my mother was always there.

Notes

The Water of Life:

Rafaello Ceccoli was an artist from Naples. From 1843 to 1852, he taught oil painting gratis at the Athens School of Art. —*Sono in pericolo, Signore*: "Sir, I'm in danger."

At the Gate to the Spring:

Selymbria Gate is also known as the Gate of the Miracles.

Balackla:

According to legend, on May 29th, 1453, a monk at Balackla was frying fish when he was informed that Constantinople had fallen to the Turks. He said that he'd only believe the City had fallen if the dead fish he was frying at that moment would jump from his pan into a nearby fountain filled with holy water. Before he finished his response, the fish leaped into the fountain and swam away.

Parthenis Visits the Monastery:

Konstantinos (Kostis) Parthenis, considered by many to be the most important Greek painter of the twentieth century, visited the Monastery of the Life-Giving Spring in 1907, where he painted seven preliminary versions of his most famous work, *The Annunciation*.

The Source of Her Tears:

Set: Sète is a port city in southeastern France. Fatima Zahra, a well-known Arab singer, would often sing at the city's annual poetry festival.

Portrait with Butterflies:

"Black Butterflies" refer, metaphorically, to the people who died on the island anonymously and have never been mentioned again. The Greek poet Miltos Sahtouris wrote poems referring to the black butterflies that come to Poros in the summer, associating them with the lives of the monks at the Monastery of the Life-Giving Spring.

—"If only you'd get TB . . .": Lyrics from a Greek Rebetika song.

—"Black Death": The last place in Greece where the Black Plague occurred was on Poros March 19, 1837.

—"Daskalio": Corruption of the Italian word "discoglio," reef, rocks near the surface of the water on nautical maps.

—"Water quick! To put out / the fires from Hell . . .": From "Twelve Lays of the Gypsy," by Kostis Palamas (1859–1943), from the summer of 1899.

Devil's Bridge:

A dangerous rock formation, known as "Devil's Bridge," that forms part of a well-known gorge along the Damalas River in the Peloponnese. The bridge gets its name from marks in the rocks that resemble the hoof prints of goats and so are associated with the Greek god Pan and the Devil.

Giannis Scarlatos and Xanthoula Kouneli:

Giannis Scarlatos (1907–1955); Xanthoula Kouneli-Scarlatou (1907–1955). All Scarlatos's paintings were stolen; as a result today few people know about him or his work.

Giannis Scarlatos's Engagement 1952:

After the death of her husband, Xanthoula Kouneli closed herself up in the family's seaside house. Scarlatos painted a still-life depicting lemon twigs in a glass of water with the painter's wedding rings placed in front of the glass.

Paint Store:

Oka: A unit of measure going back to the Ottoman Empire. One oka is about 2.75 pounds, or, as a liquid measure, 1.3 pints.

The Annunciation (1907):

See "Parthenis Visits the Monastery" above. The icon hangs in the Church of Saint George in the town of Poros.

The Month of Departures:

"Papa et mama gratia, addio, pregare per me, / 1 Septembre 1907, / il povero Kostis": "Father and Mother, thank you, goodbye. Pray for me. / September 1, 1907 / the unfortunate Kostis [Konstantinos Parthenis]."

The Fateful Summer of Ioannis Kapodistrias, 1831:

Ioannis Antonios Kapodistrias was chosen as the first head of newly independent Greece (1827–31). In 1831, a few months before his assassination in Nafplion, in the face of an impending attack by rebellious naval forces from Hydra, he travelled to Poros to organize the island's defenses.

Merçi pour le Beau Sejour:

Merçi pour le beau sejour: "Thanks for the Beautiful Stay." The thank-you note the painter March Chagall wrote in the Villa Galini guestbook after his visit there in 1952.

—Bandoneon: A type of concertina often associated with the tango.

With a View of the Sea:

Spyros Athanassiou-Sakelliou (1887–1955) is the author's paternal grandfather.

—Irini (Nina) Kontovasili Sakelliou (1905–1985) is the author's grandmother.

—Damalas: The modern name for ancient Trizina. In the time of Venetian domination it was comprised of the barony of Ntamalet and Elmala.

The Palaces:

The Palaces are another name for the Temple of Poseidon and its surrounding structures from antiquity. Demosthenes committed suicide there by drinking hemlock.

—Lines 29–34 are paraphrased from Plutarch's *Parallel Lives, Demosthenes, Vol 23*: . . .*ἐγὼ δ' ὦ φίλε Πόσειδον ἔτι ζῶν ἐξίσταμαι τοῦ ἱεροῦ· τὸ δ' ἐπ' Ἀντιπάτρῳ καὶ Μακεδόσιν οὐδ' ὁ σὸς νεὼς καθαρὸς ἀπολέλειπται.*

Vigil:

Details in this poem refer to artifacts that archaeologists found when excavating the Temple of Poseidon and the surrounding area.

Recording the Sacrifices:

Lines 66–72 are based on lyrics by C. H. Myris (Kostas Georgousopoulos) to the song "Full Moon Eros" (1991).

Galini—His Last Strait:

The Greek poet George Seferis wrote one of his best-known poems, "The Thrush," while at the Villa Galini, a residence owned by the family of his wife Maro. Prior to their marriage in 1941, Seferis would spend time there with Maro and her two daughters from a previous marriage. The third part of "The Thrush" refers to Antigone, the young protagonist of Sophocles' tragedy of the same name, who lives in a palace with abundant light, not unlike the many-windowed spacious Villa Galini.

Matina and the Story of Extermination:

Matina Kouneli-Douka (1922–1984), as an interpreter in the German headquarters on Poros, managed to save many locals from the island.

—*"Su se su su su sclaf mein Kindelein,"*: "Shhh, sleep my dear child," from *The Andernacher Gesangbuch* (Cologne 1608), a Catholic hymnbook.

Living in Silver:

Modi is a rocky island off the Cape of Kalavria, a transit point in Mycenean times.

Tselevinia:

Tselevinia (Zelevinia) is located at the eastern end of the Argolid Peninsula and is the easternmost tip of a geographical area of the same name in the Peloponnese.

Bird of Death:

In the early hours of April 21, 1967, a group of right-wing officers seized power in Greece and imposed a military dictatorship on the country for seven years.

About the Author

Liana Sakelliou has published thirty books of poetry and criticism as well as translations of Ralph Waldo Emerson, Sylvia Plath, Emily Dickinson, H.D., Denise Levertov, and Gary Snyder. Her own poems have been translated into twelve European languages—including her most recent volume of poems *Sequentiae* (2024) in Romanian, and *This Side of Eden* (2025) in Romanian and English—and have appeared in a number of anthologies and international journals.

She is Professor Emerita of the Department of English Language and Literature at the University of Athens. The recipient of grants from, among others, the Fulbright Foundation and the Department of Hellenic Studies of Princeton University, Ms. Sakelliou served as a member of the Administrative Council of the Greek Authors Society, and was Chair of the Selection Committee for the European Union Prize for Literature. *Ὅπου φυσᾶ γλυκὰ ἡ αὔρα* (The Greek original of *Wherever the Sweet Breeze Blows*) was a finalist for the Greek National Poetry Award.

About the Translator

Born in Nevada and raised in California, Don Schofield is a graduate of the University of Montana (MFA, 1980).

A resident of Greece for many years, he has taught literature and creative writing at American, British, and Greek universities and traveled extensively throughout Europe, the Middle East, and farther afield. Fluent in Greek, a citizen of both his homeland and his adopted country, he is the editor of the anthology *Kindled Terraces: American Poets in Greece* (Truman State University Press), and has published six books of poetry in the U.S., the first of which, *Approximately Paradise* (University Press of Florida), was a finalist for the 1985 Walt Whitman Award, and a more recent collection, *In Lands Imagination Favors* (Dos Madres Press), reached the final round for the 2015 Rubery Book Award (UK). His translations of contemporary Greek poets have been honored by the London Hellenic Society, shortlisted for the Greek National Translation Award and nominated for a Pushcart Prize. Six poems from his latest poetry book, *A Different Heaven: New & Selected Poems* (Dos Madres Press 2023), were also nominated for a Pushcart Prize. His memoir *From the Cyclops Cave* (Open Book Press) came out this past fall. Currently he lives in both Athens and Thessaloniki.

www.ingramcontent.com/pod-product-compliance
Lightning Source LLC
LaVergne TN
LVHW090524110826
845146LV00003B/969

* 9 7 9 8 9 0 1 4 6 7 0 2 2 *